UNTOUCHABLE

HOW TO BLOW YOUR COMPETITION OUT OF THE WATER

By
Jose M. Gonzalez Riley

To my wife, Krish, for *everything*.

Thanks Mum for reading to me before I could read, and for Think And Grow Rich. Thanks Amit for being the catalyst of the first opportunity and Brinder for many great opportunities. And thanks Jon Penberthy for a pivotal moment and for being the catalyst for this book.

INTRODUCTION

For years, I was the undisputed 'go-to' guy in the UK for one of 'The Big 5' SAAS (software as a service) ecommerce companies on the planet, up until a shift in the market and a downturn in the economy forced all of us to change direction (that is to say, *nobody* took my place).

During those 5 years, I got to work with clients in 21 different countries across 5 continents, launching over 230 online stores, countless blogs and websites, marketing some and advising many on how to grow their brands online - business owners and entrepreneurs in Japan, the US, Ireland, Canada, Israel, South Africa, Lebanon, Switzerland, Australia, UK and many other countries.

What nobody knew is that I was working alone, from my couch and from any coffee shop where I could find a wifi connection as I travelled up and down the country to visit my *then*-girlfriend-now-wife, armed with just a laptop and an outdated mobile phone with the temperament of a faulty traffic signal.

Something else they didn't know is that I wasn't an expert - far from it. In fact, in the beginning I could barely find my way around their software platform. I'd never done anything in ecommerce either. Laughably, I didn't - and still don't - have any web design qualifications. Talking of which... I left school with 1 qualification in French - not really surprising since I'd only started learning English one and a half years earlier and was still far from fluent.

But this book is not a story about achievements; nor is it a book about me. It's about *you* and your business, your brand. And it's important, because the things I did can stop *you* from getting wiped out by bigger, better, richer and more established competitors. It doesn't matter if you're a dentist, a blogger, a plumber, an Amazon seller, a gym owner, an online training provider, a coach, an accountant, an SME and anything in between.

I did it intuitively, which is another way of saying *I made a boat load of mistakes and lost a lot of money but made good in the end.* But now I have hindsight, which means I have a blueprint.

And this book is that blueprint.

So, how did I do it? Was I 'well connected?' Nope. My childhood friends are in a different country and couldn't 'be there' to pull me through doors and get me into the right places. Nor did I have the right kind of 'peers' later on. I vaguely attended secondary school during the two years since my arrival in the UK and the last day of school, and I had no idea what people were saying for most of that time. Perhaps not surprisingly then, I left school with a only couple of good friends, one of whom I still have the fortune to call one of my best friends. And whilst I did start to make friends later on, these were mostly work colleagues with whom I didn't socialise. The handful of other friendships I made along the way slowly faded, mostly because I didn't maintain them as well as I should have. So no, I can't credit the Friends Card.

So, was I better qualified than my competitors? Nope. Up until that point, I had only ever worked with around 10 local clients, setting them up with simple websites. That was the full extent of my skill and experience in this field. My competitors on the other hand were web design agencies with great portfolios and teams of people in possession of fancy certificates and accreditations. Not only were they technically superior, they were a team and I was alone.

So, was I smarter than everybody else? Well, since everybody had a 15 year head start on me (I still remember watching Sesame Street episodes aged 15 and getting excited when I learned the word 'under' and 'small'...) I was hardly what you'd call 'learned'.

So, was I in the right place? Nope. I lived in a small, non-affluent town in the North West of England, with no connections to any city and certainly no connection to London.

So, did I put myself in the right place? Nope. I hardly ever left the town, didn't network, didn't attend any events and didn't really go anywhere where my would-be-customers hang out.

So how on Earth did I do it? How did somebody with no relevant qualifications, no experience, no friends to leverage, zero visibility, zero money (in case you're wondering) get to obliterate the well-established, bigger, better and smarter competitors and become the go-to guy for a big player in a huge market?

Well, you could say there was a little good fortune involved, but that's something people who don't make things work for themselves like to use as an excuse to explain away everybody else's hard-earned success and excuse themselves in the process. Good fortune is not selective. In First World countries at least, we all pretty much have access to the same good fortune. Some are better positioned than others, financially and socially, but generally we all have access to *information*.

Note that I didn't say we all have access to the same *opportunities*. Opportunities are created by manipulating that good fortune in order to prepare oneself to act when they appear, because opportunities are not selective either. They are like doughnuts: those who are in the right place, whether by chance or by design, and have the right resources (information, money or both) can take them.

Sometimes an opportunity is right in front of you *and everybody else*, hanging like an invisible thread on a spider's web, and you can't see it because you're not ready to see it, because you haven't used the 'good fortune' that's readily available to arm yourself with the things you need in order to *see* the opportunity.

Other times, you *and others* catch sight of the invisible thread, because you're ready. But seeing is not enough. You have to take it. When somebody else takes it, others say things like *I could have done that*, or *I thought of that*.

There are opportunities in your market right now that you need to exploit in order to position yourself in a way that removes your competition. But first you need to *see* them, and to see them you need to know *where* to look. And that's what I'm about to show you.

When I saw the first opportunity, I hatched a plan to exploit it and in doing so I learned *where* to look for opportunities, which enabled me to spot them *faster*.

As I said, I wasn't better than my competition... but I saw a way to be *different*. So I got to work, *crafting that difference deliberately, piece by piece*. This is what enables me to steamroll over my competitors time and again. It's also the very thing that may cost you dearly in your own business if somebody in your niche decides to steamroll over *you*.

Is that it? Be different and win the game? Well, almost. Being different is key, but there are some things that you need to have in place to position yourself for success. Napoleon Bonaparte was different, but without his propaganda machine nobody would have ever known.

This book is about crafting that difference *and* putting in place the things you need to position yourself, your business or your brand for success today. Consider it a little 'good fortune'.

Old know-how won't serve you well, if at all. These are *fast* times. Iconic brands from yesteryear have disappeared because they believed their old know-how was all they needed. But almost everything you know is useless when you land on Mars. *Or when The Rules are new.*

Let me prove it to you...

PART 1: YOUR POSITIONING

David And Goliath, And How to Create
Your Own Money-Printing ATM Machine

The first 10 minutes of my 1 on 1 consultations are always the same, but the place is always different. I've sat in plush offices, in coffee shops, in makeshift Portakabins with cables dangling one inch above my head and even inside a vintage Ferrari.

Today, I was in a big, brightly-lit boardroom, sat on a modern, hydraulic office chair, silently swinging from left to right like a pendulum and stopping suddenly each time somebody entered the room. Did I want coffee? Yes, thank you. I run on coffee. It's important to me. I swung again, from right to left this time, as soon as the door closed.

The vast, wall-mounted screen played a constant loop of mini-videos that told the story of the company. The wait was thoughtfully designed to give me time to absorb - and be impressed by - the lavish boardroom, as well as to watch and be wowed by the videos. Every key element of the environment, from the seating to the ambient light, had been manipulated to make those who find themselves here realise that they are in the presence of a goliath, for better or for worse.

It also set the tone: the man I was about to see was important. Very important. And busy. Very busy.

Finally, The Man walked in - exactly as the last video in the current loop finished playing. I thought that was a nice touch and wondered if somebody had timed the videos and crafted The

Wait to allow enough time for viewing. Considering how the rest of the environment had been manipulated for impact, I decided that yes, the length of The Wait was precisely timed.

We shook hands and he asked me if I liked the videos. I told him that there was a typo in the third video. He was shocked, speechless, embarrassed when I pointed at the butchered word on the screen as the offending video played again.

I could have also told him that the videos had very obviously been put together by an inexperienced (cheap) freelancer instead of a professional (more expensive) videographer and that not only did the background music not match the natural tempo set by the scenes and the transitions themselves, but that the music was far too loud and completely out of synch with any and all frames.

I could have also mentioned that the endings were laughable: the music cut unexpectedly and abruptly at the end of each clip, preventing the viewer from ever entering a 'trance' state and absorbing the intended message (clearly, the freelancer thought adding a bit of random music to the background is all you do…). And lastly, I could have gone for the jugular and pointed out that the images in each slide were pixelated because they'd obviously provided them in the wrong resolution, and the freelancer had gone ahead and worked with what they'd given him anyway, possibly to secure payment as fast as possible without creating an obstacle.

Perhaps they'd blown their budget furnishing this room and had nothing left but a pittance with which to secure a cheap freelancer on the other side of the world to create the very thing that would represent their fabulous company - a trailer style video - to present to those they sought to impress. Shame on them. At least when I create a video for a client, it's something that they're proud of, or moved by (one client was almost moved to tears by the company trailer I created for his firm, which was in fact designed specifically to move the target market).

But I said none of those things. My job wasn't to put those things right, after all. At the same time, I wasn't there to experience their carefully-crafted and no doubt tried-and-tested 'impress the pants out of the outsider and let them know who's in the driving seat' routine. Especially when the show was such a classless sham. *My time is important too.*

The coffee arrived and I immediately decided not to touch it again after taking just one sip. *Freeze-dried coffee! Seriously?*

My friend Dave laughed, interrupting my account. He thought it was hilarious. I looked at him, taking a consolatory sip of real, high-altitude, single-origin, non-mechanically dried, *whole bean coffee.*

Dave was visiting me at home because business was slow for him and he had time. "Why don't you advertise," I asked him?

"Can't afford it," Dave said, taking a drink from his own cup.

"How do you know you can't afford it?" I asked him.

"I don't have the money to put into it, is what I mean," he answered.

I noticed his resolution. It was a closed case. "And I meant, how much is it costing you right now to acquire a client? How much is it costing you to make a sale?"

I saw that face again, the one I'd seen earlier, whilst visiting the goliath, when I mentioned the typo. "You need to know how much you can afford to spend to acquire a new client," I said. "And then we can devise ways to bring that cost down. But we can only do this when we know your conversion rate. By improving your conversion rate (i.e. converting more of the same visitors, without spending more money on new visitors) you automatically bring down the cost of acquiring a lead."

Dave shrugged. "I can't afford it," he said, finishing his coffee and standing up. "I'm going to do a bit of Facebook and some posts."

Dave is not unique in his predicament. He's extremely talented and few people work harder than him, but The New Rules don't reward the talented or the hard working. They only reward the smart. The good news *for all of us* is that smart can be 'hired'. If you can be - or hire - smart, *and* hard-working, then you really have a good chance to thrive. But only after you position yourself correctly in order to obliterate your competition, and once you've set up the things you need to have in place.

Metrics are *one of the things* you need to have in place. You can't scale up without knowing your numbers. Scaling up by sheer luck is not something you can repeat over and over again, so it doesn't count. If I told you I'd never driven a car before but I managed to somehow drive from my place to yours, you would never in a month of Sundays get in a car with me. If you were sane.

If you don't know how much you can afford to spend on an advertising campaign and you have no idea what ROI (return on investment) to expect from an advertising campaign, then you don't have the ability to grow your business *predictably* and *deliberately*.

Before the Internet, direct marketing giants went through an incredibly complex and organised process to measure their conversion rate as accurately as they could by using coupons and measuring response against cost. These metrics were beyond the grasp and reach of small and medium-sized business owners. But today, you and every business owner has access to online systems that can track and show you those key metrics at a ridiculously affordable price. Most business owners I've dealt with, who operate on old know-how, didn't know this piece of 'good fortune'. Now *you* do.

Brendon Burchard once said, if you're not spending 1 grand a day on advertising, you don't have a business. I would add to this that, *if you have no idea of what will happen if you put 1 grand into advertising, then there's no way on Earth that you're ever going to spend 1 grand a day on advertising.*

The best positioning in the world is not going to help you much if you don't have systems in place to track and measure *everything*.

On the other hand, once you get your sales funnel to a point where you can predictably enter 1 grand and get back a little more than 1 grand, that's what I call having your own personal money-printing ATM machine. It doesn't happen without a little testing of course (this is precisely *why* we set up systems to track and test conversions). But when you reach that point, you don't want to have a marketing budget. Instead, you want to throw everything you have into that sales funnel… because you know it's profitable.

Do you think we're ready to work together now? Then let's start with *crafting your unique position...*

How I Crushed My Competition
by Taking Over The Gaps

"We desperately need an online shop that works," the voice at the other end of the phone said. Not for the first time, I answered that I didn't deal with ecommerce. But the client was desperate - a broken cart means no business online and a hit to the business's reputation.

I finally acceded. I said I would 'see what I could do'. I was under pressure. This was my biggest client to date. I had secured regular monthly income in exchange for marketing services but now they were leveraging that as much as they could to turn the pressure screw on me to deal with their online shop.

I was nervous. I had avoided ecommerce up until now, turning down the half a dozen or so queries I had received since setting up my web design agency some 6 months ago. And now it looked like I would be forced to look at ecommerce in the eye.

It all started when I discovered that there were people making money online. It was 2005 and I decided I wanted in on 'The Internet Lifestyle'. That's when my journey began. I consumed all the information I could find, buying expensive courses - anything and everything I came across. I bought a ton of trash, as well as some good stuff.

Incidentally, I still do that today. I buy everything that crosses my path to dissect it and see if there are any gold nuggets I can use. Dave thinks I'm mad, but I keep telling him: you buy fuel for your business, I buy software for mine.

Back then, ebooks were an exploding market. Write an ebook and make money. So I did. But then I discovered that I needed a website. And so I began to learn all I could about building websites until finally I had a website for my ebook.

And then I discovered that websites don't simply appear on page 1 of Google... *you have to market them.* And so began my journey into the world of SEO (search engine optimisation). Many thousands of dollars and hundreds of hours later I was able to rank my website on page 1. Moreover, I was able to repeat the process.

That's when I experienced my first 1k month. I was hooked. But somewhere along the line, not long after those early successes, I somehow got off-track and started creating websites for local businesses.

Knowing so little and wanting to help these business owners kept me extremely busy climbing a never-ending learning curve, learning a little about business, about selling, about bookkeeping, as well as continuing my SEO education. A few months later, I expanded my services to include SEO, and that's when I secured *this* client, who now was begging me to find a solution to his broken shopping cart.

I was nervous, but I didn't want to lose a client, so I started searching for online cart providers, signing up to several. I think I managed to break every demo store I set up. Luckily, one provider offered support and with some help I finally completed the store and solved the client's problem. Everything was back on track. We were moving forward again.

That's when Amit called. Amit worked in the sales team. A smart thing they did back then was to reach out to web designers and agencies and ask them if they'd be interested in helping their clients (online store owners) because they provided the software but didn't offer a setup service. Each sales person in the company had a few go-to web design agencies and Amit was looking to expand his own cluster of web designers.

I agreed, nervously. I knew very little at that point about their software - only as much as I had been able to learn setting up a single store - but this sounded like potential regular income. I may have glossed over some details of my experience, but hey...

I heard nothing for some weeks, but I used that time to learn all I could about their software, pouring over their training materials day and night. I was positioning myself for The Opportunity. When finally I got the chance to set up one very small client, I dedicated a lot of time to her to make sure she was happy with the job, because I needed her to be happy in order to get selected again for another job.

Unbeknownst to me at the time, she had rang Amit to sing my praises for being so dedicated. Wow. This was 'good fortune'. Now that I knew this information, I knew what I had to do in order to cause that to happen again.

So I did.

The glowing review from my happy client got me a couple of other small setups, and I worked just as hard to ensure the clients were bursting with happiness by the time I was done. Predictably, this too got back to where it needed to.

Then, one day, Amit mentioned that some of the usual web designers were not available or too busy for this particular job, and so I gladly took it.

Whenever a design company's name was mentioned, I would search for their website to check them out. They all had impressive websites, with dozens of services, strong teams, glowing testimonials and portfolios that showcased their skills and validated their authority in the ecommerce space.

I sat on my couch, wondering how I - the new kid on the block who knew next to nothing - could ever beat these agencies. I didn't realise that The Opportunity had already been presented to me (read the previous paragraph and see) but I spotted it the second time around.

Amit called. *Could I possibly call a client this weekend? It's the only time the client has available and I can't get any of my usual guys to call. They don't work weekends...* Of course, I said, smiling...

There it was. People who work 9 to 5 get paid to work 9 to 5. Unless they are provided with relevant opportunities, recognition or compensation, it is rare that those workers will work for free in their own time, unless they have a very good reason to.

This was my first opportunity. These web agencies were never going to be talking to anybody over a weekend. Not a chance. And so, I made it very clear to Amit that he could depend on me calling any client on *any* day.

One key strength of the competition had suddenly become a glaring weakness: it's numbers. The company owner works around the clock and when he finally grows his business he is able to delegate making calls to his staff. The flaw in the system is that, unlike the business owner, the staff are 'restricted' to making those calls from 9 to 5 by their pay structure.

The smart business owner realises the *new need in the market* and adapts by making sure he has somebody making those calls *when the market needs them*, using any tool at his disposal - flexitime, bonuses, home working etc). When business owners don't act, *a gap appears for the smart and hungry to exploit.*

That's *where* you look for gaps. Most people look at the market trying to find gaps, but *it's the things your competition isn't doing that creates those gaps.*

Weekend calls became the norm, soon followed by evening calls as I became a more useful resource. Many of the prospects the company dealt with had day jobs themselves - they were workers who wanted to try their hand at selling online, and these people could only talk in the evening. *And I was the only one willing to fill that gap.*

Evenings, mornings before 8am, whenever and however. Word soon got around the office and Amit started to introduce me on the phone to some - and eventually all - of his colleagues, who then started calling *me* whenever a 'difficult' prospect showed up on the radar. At that point I was already the 24x7 guy. I was taking calls from Singapore at 4am and dealing with Australian clients at 10pm.

My mission was to become *indispensable*, a right-arm to everyone in the sales team. So I looked for the next gap that wasn't being serviced by my competition. Soon, I was talking not just to clients, but to *prospects* who were sitting on the fence, trying to convince them to sign up.

Some prospects require a lot of time to convince, and when you work the phones on a commission basis, you can't afford to spend all your time on a potential tyre-kicker when you could be closing other prospects. And so I began taking those fence-sitters off the sales guys… relieving them of yet another burden.

Each member of the sales team would ring me after sending me a lead to see how I had got on, to see if there was a sign of a sale. *This was another opportunity.*

I started tracking all my leads and updating each of the technical sales guys via email. Full updates, daily. Morning and evening. This meant that they didn't have to keep tabs on me - they had updates around the clock before they even asked for them, and that meant *they knew where they were at all times.*

In the meantime, my glowing testimonials from clients were amassing. I soon figured out that was was good for the sales guys was good for the clients. So I started updating the clients during their store setups, mornings and evenings, so *they knew exactly where they were at all times*. I started inviting them to ask me *anything* about their stores and the platform and I spent time with them explaining things - *another thing the sales guys no longer had to do.*

I then began creating training videos to teach new store owners how to get started, and giving those away for free. It got to the point where a lot of clients would ring the office and ask for me, believing I actually worked there. On a couple of occasions, prospects I had interacted with refused to sign up or deal with anybody until they had spoken with me first. Only *then* were they happy to sign up!

As I raised my level of service at each stage, I did so with deliberate intent. I was providing an increasing amount of value to everybody whilst getting paid, but more importantly, with each move I was positioning myself in a way that I could not be usurped. My goal was to become The Only Option.

But my close rate was poor. I had never sold anything in my life and that opportunity of selling prospects was being taken away from me slowly but surely.

Naturally, the sales team closed their prospects a fast as they could in order to secure their commissions - *they weren't handing me 'good' prospects*. So I got to work only on the hard-cases, the ones that couldn't make a decision in 20 minutes of speaking with a professional salesperson.

Luckily my need to exploit that opportunity was bigger than my excuse of not being able to sell, so I devised a way to close those hard prospects. I figured out a way that enabled me to close around 7 out of 10 and sometimes more, much to everybody's amazement.

I made a point of calling the sales office *as soon as I got the go ahead from the prospect*, to tell them that the deal was done. Each and every time. I wanted to be the voice on the other end of the call, delivering the good news, always.

One particular day, I got a call from one of the sales guys who was passing me a lead that he thought was impossible. Within 3 minutes I called him back and told him the prospect was ready to buy. It was the fastest-ever close - and *that* got around the office just as fast. My name was echoed throughout that office, and I'd never set foot inside it - I had in fact, at that point, never even seen any of them in person or otherwise. And yet I was The Man of The Moment. I remember the manager telling the sales team to 'use me as a selling tool'. With my positioning, I had created an opportunity at *their end*, and they didn't miss it when it appeared. It was a two-sided opportunity in which everybody got to win.

It took me about 6 months to achieve this positioning, and once I was there, I worked smart for over 4 years to develop complementary services for those store owners that the company didn't offer, creating new opportunities along the way, until circumstances in the market changed unexpectedly and the company was forced to change direction. It was the end of an era, but it was the making of this book.

To this day, I've never told anybody what I did to close those leads.

Would *you* like to know?

It's rather simple. In the beginning I would call each lead - as instructed - and find resistance. The leads were always defensive, and it wasn't hard to figure out why. Don't you hate it when an unknown number calls your personal phone and upon answering you discover that it's somebody you've never met trying to sell you something? I figured they did too. So I started asking the sales guys for the lead's email address. I would then email the lead, explaining that I had been asked to get in touch with them. Note how I was shifting the responsibility to a 3rd party but also raising my own authority by saying that *I had been asked*. I would then briefly explain that I worked with clients in many countries setting up stores. If the lead happened to be from a country I had already worked with, I always mentioned this too. Oddly, it seems to carry the same weight than somebody declaring they're from the same golf club as somebody else - as if that were a character reference. So I used this fact every time the opportunity presented itself.

My final 'piece' was to give the lead my number and invite *them* to call *me*. When they did finally call me, it was *they* who were catching *me* by surprise, and the difference in their tone was striking. Furthermore, any pitch I made was suddenly OK, because *they* had called me, which somehow implied they were in control.

But how did I actually close them, sometimes in under 5 minutes? Well, that was the easiest part, once I was able to get around the resistance issue. The company had a 30 day money back guarantee... *which I fully exploited.* I would simply make the prospect a proposition: *sign up for the store and I will set up a dozen products for you at no cost whatsoever. This will enable me to walk you through the system and you can see how it all works. If you don't like it, you can cancel and get your money back within 30 days, and since I'm not going to charge you anything... you don't lose anything!*

It was a total no-brainer. And it made me a superstar.

And to my credit, people rarely cancelled, just as I had expected. My risk was calculated: by setting up some of their products and getting on the phone with them, I was able to make them *experience* what it would be like to have their own online store, with *their own products*. When you try to force a store on somebody, you get resistance. But when you *give them* a store and *then* try to take it off them, *the resistance works the other way.*

On many occasions, clients actually rang the sales office (after they had become clients) and thanked them for passing them on to me. This was one of the unexpected bonuses that came from providing such a high level of attention and service, because a resource that very quickly turns non-buyers into raving fans of your brand is a resource you'd be crazy to let go.

And there it is: the secret. I was simply working with whatever was available to me, discovering and then exploiting the gaps that the competition were ignoring or unable to service. Once I realised the gaps are created by the competition, it was a case of looking for where I could provide value that nobody else was providing all across the chain.

Ultimately, beating my competition was all about positioning. I became a *unique* service provider by providing a service that nobody else could *or would* provide, thus *eliminating my competition.*

I had no competitors. That's the real secret.

Dave was impressed when I revealed this to him. "But it won't work for me," he told me.

"Really?" I said. "Why is that?"

"Because," he explained. "I do what I do. I can't be different, and I can't do it differently. The job is the job."

"Ah," I said. "That's where you're wrong, my friend. You can remove your competition very quickly and create a very strong position for yourself, once you figure out how."

And that's exactly what I'm going to show you in the next chapter.

How to Eliminate Your Competition And Simultaneously Attract a Chunk of The Market by Repositioning Yourself to Become Untouchable

Dave is a stubborn person, and he doesn't take advice lightly. You see, he's built his business the hard way. He didn't have a helping hand, somebody to hold the door open for him. No. He had to fight tooth and nail for everything he has today. He earned it.

I have huge respect for Dave, and because of this, I'm not allowed to interfere. I'm not allowed to walk into his business and start mapping out a new, optimised sales funnel with an end-to-end online strategy to capture leads, measure conversion and improve ROI.

I would love to, but I can't.

The real problem is that I've known Dave for many years, and nobody likes their buddy telling them how to do something they've been doing for years. The irony is that, if Dave paid the fee to get a consultant like me to redesign his strategy from the ground up, he'd be all eyes and ears. It's a mixture of white coat syndrome and the fact that when you pay for something, you pay attention.

What Dave doesn't see right now, is that my job is not really to change a business. I'm not taking anything away - I'm *adding*. I don't sit down with business owners to tell them how to run their empires, or tell them that they're doing something wrong. I'm not the enemy. On the contrary, I'm there to stop them from getting wiped out by the real enemy: *the competition*. I'm there to tune things up, mostly so that they can get into the online space.

Now… *the online space…* that's where I know where the levers and switches are. I can set up the systems that measure and track ROI, and give them nice flashy screens with numbers that measure the pulse of their business day-to-day, so they know exactly where they are; I can craft and execute marketing campaigns and show them results down to the penny, then work on their conversion until we create The ATM Machine. And *that's the value I bring to a business owner.*

"But I already have a website," Dave explains. "I'm already online."

"Having a pizza shop in the middle of the desert and saying *I already have a pizza shop, I'm already in business*, is ignoring the big picture," I answer.

Dave shrugs.

"How much business does your website bring you?" I ask him. "What's the conversion…"

"Not that again!" Dave complains. I put my hands up. It's fine. We can talk about business, but not about *his* business.

"You said you can't change your positioning," I say, sitting back in my seat.

"That's right," Dave says. "I do what I do, and it's the same as all my competitors. I can't change what the job *is*."

"I'm going to start a new business," I announce, suddenly.

Dave looks at me, frowning.

"I'm going to launch a taxi service."

"You haven't got a clue about running a taxi service!" he laughs.

"Well," I say. "I know the town, so at least I can get people to their destination."

He squeals, almost spilling his coffee. "You mean *here*? You want to start a taxi service *here*? Dude, there's at least 3 big taxi firms here already! And they've been going for years!"

"Ah," I say. "So I have competition then."

"You do, and you don't own the market. The big 3 are already servicing that market. In fact, supply and demand is maxed out. Saturation. There's no room for another taxi service because *there's nobody left to service*."

"Then I have no choice but to steal some of the market," I say.

"You won't," Dave says. "Why would people swap their trusted taxi service for a new one? They don't *need* a new taxi service. And they're loyal to their own."

"But are the big 3 loyal to the market?" I ask.

"What?"

"Gaps," I answer. "There are always gaps that the competition creates by failing to cover them."

"You've lost me," Dave says.

"Well," I say, "since the market is already being serviced, I don't stand a chance if my positioning is *the same* as the competition. In fact, if we're all the same, then unless I'm the cheapest in the market, then there really is no reason to buy from me. And being the cheapest is the worst possible positioning you could ever take unless you have the capital to ride out a price war."

"Now you're getting it," Dave winks. "Getting people from A to B is *what it is*. You can't change the job".

"I have no intention of doing that," I tell him. "I'm changing my position."

"Even if you do, you don't have a fleet of cars. You can't compete."

"I can probably get started with 2 or 3 cars," I say.

Dave laughs again. "Then, even if you could have your pick of the market, you can only ferry some of them around, not all of them!"

"Now you're getting it," I smile. "My taxi service is for *women only*."

Dave looks at me. "What?"

"I cater only to women."

Dave shifts in his seat. He wants to say that the competition already taxis women around, but he's not stupid and he can sense there's *something* that may have potential in front of him. There's a certain appeal in exclusivity, and the competition doesn't have *that*.

"So I need less cars," I say. "At least to start with. And yes, the competition already cater to women, but not *exclusively*. The environment inside my cars will be feminine, as inclusive as I can make it to cater to different types of women. The *experience* I will provide will be a talking point. It will get shared naturally by my customers. When a woman steps off my taxi and walks into her workplace, she'll be telling her friends about the experience. That will create powerful *and free* viral marketing as well as curiosity. Other women will want to try the service.

I will of course have female drivers. They will wear a distinctive uniform too, unlike the taxi drivers of the competition who turn up in their day clothes and have no distinctive clothing that identifies them as a professional driver. When you step into a taxi, you feel like somebody off the street pinned a badge on their shirt pocket and sat behind the wheel. Inside my taxis however, my customers will be given the 'airline experience', with a chocolate at the end of the journey and an upsell: *would you like to book a ride back?*"

Dave nods and smiles. "Ok, I'm listening."

"My cars will be painted in a very distinctive way," I explain. "I will have professional signage that creates *instant visual marketing*, so even the women that have not heard about my service will become aware of the service when they see one of my cars. And the loyalty they had for their old provider will suddenly be questioned, because by catering exclusively to them, I will be exposing the fact that the old provider is not really catering to *them* at all. Everything I add to their experience is a stark reminder of what the competition isn't doing for them. They will suddenly see that their sense of loyalty is largely a one-way-street. The old provider was providing a service that they needed, so they really had no choice but to use it. Until now, that is. I on the other hand will provide transportation, plus safety, plus a pleasant and stylish environment that caters to them, plus exclusivity."

"And a chocolate at the end of it all," Dave chimes in.

"And an upsell," I agree. "And many of those women have children. Do you think they may be interested in my school-ride service? A service that only caters for school runs? Again, with the right environment for those customers? Perhaps I'll have a minivan that provides that service. But I will let my customers tell me, by asking them whether they would use that service and what they would want that experience to be like for their children."

"Ok," says Dave. "You got me there. That was a good one. You entered a crowded market and made yourself unique."

"Indeed," I nod. "But it's a little more powerful than that. What I actually did was to *remove the competition.* This gives me the ability to improve my margins. Price is not an issue when you're the only one offering the service. How big or how rich my competitors are becomes irrelevant because I sidestepped them."

Dave sits back, thinking. Nodding to himself. "Positioning," he says.

I nod back.

"So how would you be able to help a dentist?" he asks. "They can't really only cater to women - everybody has teeth?"

I smile. "Why can't a dental boutique cater only to women?"

Dave shrugs. "I don't know if that's a good idea... I mean,

everybody has teeth. They'd be ignoring 50% of the market…"

"There are variables you can play with when it comes to your positioning," I answer. "It doesn't have to be just about the offer. With a dentist, I would start looking at where the points of differences can be created, starting from the waiting room. Every dental waiting room looks the same - some plusher than others, but generally a waiting room is a waiting room. This is an opportunity to think outside the box and create a new experience by tweaking the environment. Imagine if you walked into a dentist and the waiting room was the inside of a mouth, and the chairs were teeth".

Dave laughs out loud. "That's ridiculous!"

"What would you be talking to me about right now, if you'd just come back from that dentist?"

"I'd be telling you about me sitting inside a mouth," Dave laughs.

"And I'd be making an appointment right there and then, just to see what you saw," I say.

"That's a bit extreme," Dave says, still laughing.

"But you're still thinking about it," I say. "It's not an experience one forget easily. Imagine if you were a kid, and your dentist's waiting room was a mouth…"

Dave laughs again. "I'd be in the dentist every day!"

"And raving about it to your friends," I add.

"Ok," Dave says. "So you can tweak the environment."

"Yes. That *was* an extreme example, but the point was that *you control the experience*, so it makes little sense to offer the same experience everybody else is offering. But still, that's only one variable. Your point of difference could be something else: maybe as a dentist you have worked on celebrities' teeth, or you've been on tv, or you've authored a book. Maybe you have an app where all your customers can consume your content, your tips, as well as your offers... In the early days of the Web, having a website was a point of difference. Apps are not new, but most businesses still don't leverage that opportunity.

All those things are points of difference that you can *and should* exploit in order to separate yourself from your competition. The more you can separate yourself from the enemy the less they can reach you. And when you do this properly, when you craft your points of difference well, the competition ceases to exist."

Dave nods thoughtfully.

"You're still vulnerable to outside factors like the economy, the market's needs changing, rent, etc, *but so is your competition*. That's just the atmosphere in which all businesses operate. But as long as the atmosphere is good for you to operate in, then you don't have the worry of your competitors coming out with better offers and stealing your market - because you're providing a unique *something* that can't be bought somewhere else."

"What about online?" Dave says. "How would this work online?"

"The Web enables you to reach even more people with your offer, but your competition usually increases exponentially, so you still need to have those points of difference. If you're a betting expert and you launch a website for people who bet, you're entering a market dominated by big players. So instead, identify a segment of that market and then position yourself to serve only that segment in a way that nobody else does or can. For example, if you discovered that students make up a % of the market, then your website could be a betting site for students. Now you have something to work with.

Your positioning is the result of all the points of difference that you craft into your offer. Cater to those students in a unique and exclusive way whilst providing them the result they wanted in the first place and you've won them. Your unique positioning will make them aware that the big betting sites are providing the service they want but not really catering to them specifically. Your website on the other hand will make them feel like they're a part of something special, that they are *understood*. And that's powerful."

"And if you cut grass?" Dave asks.

"It's digital," I answer. "You don't need to cut the grass online".

"No, I meant if your job is cutting grass…"

"My mother's gardener has unique positioning," I answer. "There's a ton of landscape gardeners around here, and I see tree-cutting and grass-mowing vans almost daily in Summer. And yet, everybody in my mother's street uses the same gardener."

"So he's good then," Dave says.

"No," I answer. "He crafted a unique point of difference. He can't drive - in fact, he drags his lawn mower behind him up and down the street. He's not great at communicating either. He's uneducated, his vocabulary is limited, he's clearly not a sales person and there's nothing sophisticated about him. And yet, I watch him like a hawk when I see him, because he single-mindedly demolished his competition - much brighter and experienced people with fleets of vehicles."

Dave nods. He has seen him too, dragging that lawn mower up and down the place.

"He knocked on my mother's door one day and asked if she wanted him to cut the grass. He had all his tools with him there and then, so she agreed. Not only did he do a great job, but he then secured his next visit before he left.

That was 4 years ago. He continued to service that garden up until last year, every fortnight during summer and every 6 weeks during winter, lawn mower in tow. His service was convenient and affordable, and it created natural word-of-mouth advertising.

In over 20 years that my mother has lived in her house, nobody has ever knocked on the door and asked if she'd like the grass cut."

"So what happened last year" Dave asks.

"It all came crashing down on him," I answer. "He went into a bigger market - tree-cutting - a market where he wasn't unique. I'm not entirely sure what happened to him, but he's recently started doing the rounds again, cutting grass - only this time, he's really having to sell himself, because he let down his tribe, the people he was serving. He abandoned them, and people remember that. Even though nobody has replaced his service in all this time, people are not that open to him this time around. He didn't show loyalty to his market."

Dave looks thoughtful.

"He had started to build something great," I continue, "a recurring income with zero-cost marketing after his initial effort. But that was only the beginning. He exploited the first gap: the fact that the competition - for some reason - don't knock on doors and don't put leaflets through doors.

His second masterly move was to secure an open-ended schedule of further visits. The market was happy and he was getting paid doing what he does.

But the competition could still have turned up, with their gleaming vans, and undercut him on price. If you have competition, that means you don't really have a strong enough point of difference, and when your competition starts to poach your customers, you depend entirely on your customer's sense of loyalty toward you. And that can be put to the test and used against you if the competition is smart. Just like I showed with my fictitious taxi service."

Dave nods.

"Let's say the competition hired me to do just that: to usurp the gardener's position. Let's summarise the job...

How to Take Over Your Market if You're a Medium Size Player With Some Resources

Here's what I would do:

1. Start knocking on doors. We match the gardener's approach because he proved it worked. That saves us time and money testing the best approach.

2 . Turn up in uniforms (not jeans and a t-shirt). No matter how small the job is, if the provider doesn't show that he or she is taking pride in the job, then somebody else will. Dress up for the occasion. This conveys efficiency.

3. Turn up in a group of 2 or 3 and explain to the customer what it is that you offer (don't ask if they want their grass cutting, but tell them *how* you deliver your service - *the experience*). A group of people conveys speed, organised work, trustworthiness.

4. Present a visual plan. Have one leader in the group, carrying a smart tablet or a clipboard - something they can show. Don't sell invisible things. Show photos of other work and - for a conversion booster - show videos of smiling customers in their gardens, next to the smiling, uniformed group of workers, saying how they *feel* about their garden. Show that you have a plan that includes a schedule and packages to choose from - weekly, fortnightly or monthly. Show also the most popular package.

5. Give a free demo. The first grass cut is on the house. But it can't be done there - they have to book a day. This will enable

them to experience the whole thing from the start. I want the customer to get a courtesy call one day before the appointment, firstly to enquiry if they are well, and secondly to make sure that the appointment is still on. This reduces potentially wasted trips but also keeps us fresh in the customer's mind.

Then, I want the customer to see the gleaming vans turn up in the morning. Clean, sparkling. I want the team leader to knock on the door and greet the customer *before a single tool is taken out of the van.* I don't want the customer to open her front door and see a bunch of people dragging noisy machines down her front path. We don't take the customer for granted. We want permission to enter. Always. Only then, after the team leader greets the client, does the team enter. The customer is paying their wages - I want each member of the team to greet the customer. If anybody in the team is a grumpy pants, they're out of a job. It's that simple. Weak links in a company are what brings a company down. The employee with the attitude is the source of the complaints.

So… next, the team leader is going to ask the customer if there are any tasks - or anything - they need to consider or be aware of (like, *don't touch that mint plant!*). Don't assume what the job is. The hairdresser knows the customer wants a haircut, but they still ask *how*. And finally, after the job is done and the garden has been tidied, the team leader asks the customer to step out and inspect the work. Do we get a yes? Great. Out comes the clipboard, the signed-off sheet - *branded with the company logo and services* - the small gift: a mug, with the company's logo and telephone number, and 2 postcards: one that has the website address and more information, and the other showing a half price offer for the next 3 visits *when you take up a maintenance plan*, plus a free garden preventative maintenance consultation to help them plan against the coming Winter and potential issues (like overgrown trees). Do not sell to the customer, unless the customer asks there and then to book a plan. As soon as the team are back in the vans, ring the office and have somebody call the customer - a courtesy call to check that all went well and would they like to book a maintenance plan? Not right now? No problem. *The postcard the team leader handed you has the website address with the packages, and you can still call us anytime.*

6. The price point will be very affordable for the first 3 to 6 visits. Half price in fact. It's a great way for the customer to save, and a great way for the service provider to introduce the customer to the experience.

7. We sit down at the end of each run and analyse the conversion rate. Those that didn't convert are the ones I'm most interested in. Why didn't they convert? What was the obstacle and how can it be removed? Can we survey the customer and find out what we can do to remove that obstacle?

8. We tweak the approach after the data is crunched. We amplify what works and remove what doesn't.

9. We go to work on the next neighbourhood, and we start to leverage the previous successes by telling the new prospects how many new customers in this area have *just joined us* in the

past few days. Recency is important. We are a new phenomenon and we are 'happening' and you better join us now or miss out and be left out of this fantastic experience we and all your friends are enjoying.

10. We introduce our 'custom' plan to new customers after the first 3 visits. Not everybody likes to have worksheets signed off in their face at the end of each job - some people want a friendlier touch. We want to sit down with each client and understand them so that we can tailor the experience to *them*.

11. We discover what else our clients have issues with. Need to pull down and take away that old shed? Need a new one? Need trees cutting? Then we expand our services or we subcontract those out - but only after vetting any and all subcontractors personally, making it very clear to them that one single screw up and they're out. Do not sign long term contracts with people you don't know. Every subcontractor you send into your customer's garden is representing *you* and your brand, *not their own*. Your customer doesn't care what the grumpy subcontractor that shouted at her dog's problem is. It's *your* fault. Protect your hard-earned customers. If you can't be there to manage the experience, call the customer as soon as the subcontractor leaves to find out if they were treated well. Deal with any issue immediately.

12. Keep a close eye on your subcontractors. If they can see what you're doing, they can attempt to model it. It's best if you can manage those new services in-house, but if you must subcontract then ensure to guard against prying eyes.

13. Start collecting your customers' emails after week 3, ready for phase 2 (this will bring down the cost of marketing significantly). But don't ask for their email. Instead, make it convenient for them to get in touch with you by giving them your email, and invite them to enter into a raffle (e.g a free garden makeover or one free session or something suitable).

14. Create an incentive for your customers to recommend your service to their friends and family. This will bring your cost of lead acquisition to zero and help you expand your customer base faster.

15. Start expanding your services by cross-selling. Your customers have gardens and you are already in those gardens. Sell garden furniture, plant pots, awnings, swings, solar lights, bbq equipment, gazebos and anything else that you can conceive of.

16. Become The Indispensable Go To in your market.

How well do you think we may do with that strategy?" I ask Dave.

Dave nods, thoughtful..

"You can take any of those concepts and apply them in your business," I add.

"So what if instead,"Dave says, "the lone gardener hired you to protect himself against his competition?"

This time, I laugh. "You're putting me to the test?"

"I just saw how a bigger company with resources can take over the market and crush the little guy. But now I want to see how a small one person company with no resources and all the odds against them can do the same."

"Ok," I say. "Let's save the gardener..."

How to Take Recover From a Screw Up And Take Back Your Market if You're a One Person Company With Few Resources

If I were hired by the gardener to fix his issues, here's what I would tell him:

1. Get some custom-made postcards that promote your revamped service, but have them say SORRY. We're going to start with an apology. Abandoning your tribe and then coming back a year later and asking to *pick up where you left and would they like to book now…* is tactless, to say the least.

2. Visit a couple of days after the apology card. Ask them how they have been - you're not the only person with a story. Take an interest in your customers. Through their stories, they're going to tell you *how* you can serve them. But more than that, you may learn a few things by listening to people's stories. When you do speak, don't lie. Yes you did do some work elsewhere, and that required you to leave your market. It was a lot better paid (nobody can hold that against you) but it wasn't for you. You're entitled to try things and try to earn your worth, and it's unavoidable to make mistakes. The important thing is to recognise the mistakes and step up to them.

3. The offer: you're going to offer a free session. Cut the grass, tidy things up. Do what you do best, for free. But not right there and then - remember: set up the experience. You will need to return. Today is just about knocking on doors and speaking with the old customers. Batch your tasks to be more efficient.

4. Get some business cards. (One thing that the gardener does to this day is shove broken bits of paper through the letterbox whenever he misses his client. It looks terrible).

5. Start being punctual. (One pet hate amongst his clients is that they have to wait in for him to appear dragging his mower behind him. But he wouldn't know this, because he never thought to ask his customers).

6. Survey your customers. Ask: if you could have the old service back, what would you change, or add? Take note and don't be stupid enough to take offence, because those who answer are going to give you the very key to *creating a custom service for them.*

7. Turn up, with your new uniform: a t-shirt, professionally printed, with *I'm Your Friendly Gardner - Just Ask* or *Need a Gardener? Just Ask!* And get used to wearing that t-shirt everywhere you go, especially in places where you have to queue up.

8. Do your job and do it well. Over-deliver, especially in this free session. When you're done, take a photo of the garden from the very best angle (use your smartphone).

9 - Ask the customer to step outside and inspect the work. Is there anything else you can do? *Would you like me to move anything for you while I'm here? It's not a problem.* Then, after the customer is happy, ask if they would like to sign up again to the old plan. Not right now? Not a problem. Here's my business

card - you have my number - just call me when you need me (not 'if', but 'when') and I will be happy to pop over.

10. If the customer agrees to the plan, get that photo of their garden printed onto a postcard and have your website (you don't have a website? *Get one!*) and details of your new service (see next point) on the other side. Give the card to the customer next time you see them. This is your calling card, but it's personalised to them. They're not going to put a crappy card on display... but they may put a photo of their garden looking its best on display, and that is a reminder (for them) to book a trim when the garden starts to get out of hand, as well as a free advert for you when visitors gather in your customer's home.

11. Buy a new, cheap, throwaway mobile phone (not a smartphone) and get a pay-as-you-go SIM card. This is your new business number (the same one that's printed on your new advertising t-shirts and business cards). Keep that phone on you at all times.

12. Introduce your 2 packages (don't do any more than two). Package 1: standard service (everything you did for them in the old service - *don't take away anything they had before*) and package 2: custom (higher priced) service. In this package you're going to include trimming the trees, painting and coating the garden fence twice a year, etc. You need to separate the service with the extras to make it clear it costs more to do those extra things.

Offer a text-service to *all customers*. They can text you when they need something - *anything* - and you'll turn up. Give examples: moving tree branches that the wind brought down, fixing the fence panel that the wind blew off etc. Position it as a text-on-demand service. Come up with a snazzy name (Text-The-Gardener or anything else) and make this the core of your message (include it on your t-shirts). Note however that you should set the expectation of a 24 hour turnaround, because you can't currently service that demand. More on this later.

13. Get a menu of your new services presented individually (not as part of a package) printed professionally, branded, with your website address and your phone number. These services include fence painting, moving rubbish, clearing branches etc. Your Custom package will include many of those services (like fence upkeep) but this menu is for the customers who stay on the basic package - they still need their fences painting and protecting, it's just that they don't want to be paying a higher recurring fee. So offer those services a-la-carte. *And remind them that you are one text away.*

14. Start looking at the weaknesses in your chain of delivery. We fixed the crappy messaging with business cards, but your punctuality stinks. Start looking at either friends or family or a taxi service or a bike with a trailer or at some way that suits your environment and gets you to work fast and punctual. You're servicing the entire street in one day and taking an hour to get there and back. This is idiotic and seeing you dragging that machine behind you at the end of the day, covered in sweat, is not an inspiring advert. Go crazy and hire a drop off and a pick up for that day. Act professional.

15. Start interacting with your customers to find out how you can personalise your service. Start retraining your customers to ask you to do things they need. My mother always needs things moving around in the garden and the gardener has never introduced the idea to her that he could be doing those things. These are all extras that can be charged for.

16. Start a newsletter or get used to printing and delivering postcards where you can advertise upcoming 'events' ahead of time. *Next month, I'm going to be painting fences and preparing them for Winter. Would you like me to add you to the list so I can come prepared?* Mention the 'event' next time you work the garden. Remind them that they need to book this or they will miss out, because you won't be painting fences again until Spring. This adds urgency to your offer and creates a feeling of missing out (as long as they need the fence painting, of course). Doing this will enable you to expand your services, remove other competitors before they remove *you* and more importantly, it will enable you to batch your jobs. You can turn up on the day with paint and brushes and service all the fences in the area *instead of doing it in bits and pieces.*

17. Start an incentive program. Recommend family and friends and get (...) free. This brings your cost of lead acquisition to zero and grows your customer base faster.

18. Expand your services. Start talking to garden centres, flower shops and wholesalers. What can you buy - products and service - to add to your value chain? Garden gnomes? Garden furniture? Where are your customers going to buy garden accessories? Do

these places offer a referral system? No? Then ask if they will. When I lived in Spain as a kid, my friends' mother was a travel guide. She would command dozens of tourists at any one time, taking them around the town. There were two cinemas in town... she would stroll up to one and ask: *why should I bring my 20 customers in here, and not the other cinema?* Cinemas don't run referral programs... *until you ask them when your tribe is ready to buy.* Walk into a garden centre with your business card and your t-shirt and make it clear that you have a paying customer base and that you're looking to add value to them. Start to form partnerships with local suppliers of anything relevant, from compost to pebbles and rocks. Become the Go To guy for your customers.

19. The next time you even *think* about going into a different market, put in place the things and people you need to continue servicing the mini empire you've built, otherwise it will go to ruin.

"I see what you did there," Dave interrupts. "You started exploiting the gaps that the bigger competitors have created."

"Exactly!" I answer. "It's too expensive for a bigger company to offer that level of attention to a single client - especially the text-on-demand service. And our gardener can exploit this gap. The competitor's strengths are sometimes their weaknesses too. A bigger boxer is stronger, but being bigger can also mean being slower. A bigger company usually has more resources, but they can also be less flexible and less responsive because of their size."

"Identify the gaps in the market," Dave says, "but don't look at the market for gaps… *the gaps are created by the competition, not the market!*"

"I couldn't have put it better myself," I smile.

"So even with fewer resources, you can take on and beat the competition when you identify the gaps they're leaving," Dave muses.

"Don't let the competition's resources blind you. Imagine you're an out-of-work mechanic, knocking on doors, trying to get some work that way…"

"Aha!" Dave almost jumps out of his seat, startling me. "*That* wouldn't work! If somebody knocked on my door and asked me that… I'd say no. I take my car to the garage."

"So do I," I reply. "Except for that time - years ago - when my car broke down and I had to call *you* to tow me back because I had no breakdown cover."

Dave narrows his eyes, sensing that I've found a gap.

"Garages have more resources, yes, but they can't usually provide a customised *mobile* experience, because they're tied down to one location. This is a gap to be exploited. Our mechanic has one car and a few tools. So… invest in professional branding and car signage, then drive out to a business park and start pushing leaflets through those office doors. Then drive out in the morning, before anybody gets there, and park your car at the entrance where everybody has to drive past it and see the signage. Make sure you're in a place where cars can pull in, and make yourself visible. Stand outside your car with your coffee, and wear that t-shirt / uniform that identifies you as the professional.

Do you know the amount of times I've worked in an office over the years, and had to take my car to a nearby garage to deal with something unexpected? From a stuck window wiper to a knocking sound, to a bust light to a punctured tyre. It cost me around two hours of my time to deal with this, and that included having to find the garage. If I had seen a mobile mechanic parked at the entrance of the business park, I'd have been all over him.

But that's only the beginning. Put leaflets on every car when people are at work. Venture into the reception and introduce yourself and leave a leaflet there too.

Talk to business owners and introduce a maintenance plan where you can service people's cars whilst they are at the office. This is hugely convenient for them - it means they don't have to lose time - they are already at the office and their car needs are taken care of.

Then expand your services: survey your customers. What else do they want? Car valeting? Invest in a machine.

Then create your incentives plan. Then provide a range of branded accessories... then take on a second person and hit two locations at once. Have a text-on-demand service. Text-a-Mechanic."

"I get it, I get it," Dave says. "It's just about finding the gaps. I see now. But tell me, this works the same way online?"

"Yes. Better still, online the playing field gets levelled, which plays to your advantage. Online you have the same tools at your disposal than your competition: a website, social media, video, etc. But most small business owners don't leverage this at all. They get a website and they believe that's the box ticked. *They don't realise that's where it all starts*. So they end up with a desperately out-of-date website and no online strategy to grow their brands, whilst the smart competitors utilise all the tools they can to scale rapidly.

At the very least, you should be using the web to generate extremely cheap leads and to measure your ROI. If you're based online anyway, then your costs are significantly cheaper - you can generate your leads online and send them to your offers whilst measuring your conversion rate very accurately. This enables you to know your cost of sales, which is a tremendously powerful metric.

You also need to be building up your relationship with your audience, and online you can do this so much more effectively. But you need the right systems in place to deliver your messages and to track and see whether those messages are being opened and what the response is."

"You can do that online?" Dave looks surprised.

"Yep. You can do *magic* online. And if your business is offline, you can - *and must* - leverage that magic to promote your brand and generate new business. The gardener, the mechanic, the dentist, the taxi service *all* need to be online, providing more value to their customer base but also promoting their brand to generate new leads and tracking everything down to the penny in order to scale."

Dave looks at his hands. Then at me, thinking hard.

"I can see you still have some questions," I say.

Dave nods. "My mind is on fire," he admits. "But I have a problem applying this thinking *to my situation.*"

"I'll tell you what," I say. "Let me make a coffee and then I will *destroy* these silly ideas that you have. I will *prove* to you that those ideas you currently hold are *false.* Deal?"

FALSE: I'm Scared That if I Ignore Most of My Market and Focus on Just a Segment, I May Hurt My sales...

Any seasoned business owner will tell you that you can't serve everybody unless you're selling toilet paper or coffins.

Your customers are not equal. Some spend more with you than others, and some (usually the ones that spend the least) leech all your time and resources. By trying to serve everybody you're doing yourself and your best customers a disservice and stopping your brand from scaling.

When I first started out selling SEO (search engine optimisation) I was excited because *every website needs SEO in order to rank in the search engines*. This seemed like a dream come true. It was the perfect market. Every website owner wants their website to be found online. That's usually the first objective of a website.

But I couldn't have been more wrong. What I soon realised is that my new website clients typically had no idea of what SEO is. They thought that a website would just (somehow) appear in the top spot of Google. They assumed that their new website would 'just' knock down the competitors, who already had websites, and they would reign supreme.

It didn't occur to them that if this is how ranking worked, websites would cost an enormous amount of money, because you would be guaranteed the number 1 spot in Google (i.e. massive exposure for your brand, not to mention a lot of revenue). So, why would a web designer charge a small one-time fee for a website that was going to automagically rank and bring in a tsunami of business? They wouldn't of course, and neither would you if you had that ability.

Personally, I would create websites only for insurance companies in every city of the world, and they would then all be number 1 in Google and I would rent each website to the highest bidder then retire to my own paradise island. And then I would lose my entire fortune the moment somebody else created a new insurance website, because *their website* would magically be the number 1 website.

It became obvious that I needed to educate the new clients on how SEO works. The problem with this, is that it takes a lot of resources to educate somebody, and it's a risky business model when you have no idea whether the client - once you've spent all that time educating them - will go ahead and buy your service. But I didn't see it at the time, and continue to burn up my resources educating everybody.

Then, one day, I had a new prospect on the phone - he had seen my website, liked the sound of my testimonials, and contacted me. He was an online retailer, running his own online shop, and had employed SEOs in the past. Various agencies in fact. He was disappointed with the results that he'd had so far and was wondering if I could help him.

I jumped on his site whilst we were on the phone and went through the immediate issues I could see. There were conversion killers everywhere. I could also see that there had been no real thought behind the website structure and as a result there were leaks all over the place. I provided an immense amount of value on the phone for a full hour, without charging anything, and as soon as we were done, he hired me on the spot. I worked with that client for over 5 years - right up until I shifted my business model and began working the ecommerce space.

What I discovered during that phone call, is that my ideal customer was *somebody who had experienced SEO already but was not happy with their results*. This brought my costs down tremendously by not having to spend a serious amount of time educating the prospect. It also improved my ROI tremendously, because I wasn't having to 'sell' SEO. They already knew what SEO was, so I could focus on selling my service, which was based on my experience.

When you buy a car, your choices are about which brand you want, what style you like most. The sales person doesn't have to educate you on *what a car is*. By trying to serve everybody, I had been spending all my time educating clients on what SEO is, and *only then* they were deciding whether this was something to try or not. Trying to serve everybody is a huge waste of your time and *it stops you from making money by providing real value to those customers who need it*. Don't do it.

And if you *do* try this, because you think that your offer is 'different', then realise this: you will never get paid what your service is worth by targeting clients who are not an ideal match. Imagine I show you a painting, and you think that the painting is terrible, almost offensive. I then tell you that the painting is worth

$3 million. Are you wrong? Or are you right? Are the art critics wrong? Or are *they* right?

Now imagine, that you *do* appreciate art, and you get your hands on a $20 million Picasso. *Try selling it to an Eskimo.*

Is the Eskimo wrong for thinking it's worthless?

The only answer that matters is that *it doesn't matter.* The truth is that in all those examples, *the prospects were not the right match.*

When I did sell SEO services to those clients who had no idea what SEO was, and I achieved the near-impossible, they had no idea what I had just done (and how much *that* was worth). And often times when I quoted a non-SEO savvy client, they would only look at the price tag and huff... not understanding the amount of work and skill involved in what they were actually asking me to achieve for them.

On the other hand, working with clients who appreciated how complex SEO can be brought many rewards, for both me *and* them. My successes were celebrated and my service was appreciated, which positioned me as a huge asset to their business. This secured recurring business and enabled me to provide even more value.

It also saved me a huge amount of stress, not having to deal with unrealistic request, like the time I had a client with a joke of a website who wanted to be number 1 in Google for 'designer bags' and was 'willing' to spend £500.

Hah!

These days I have 'filters' to filter out the wrong clients, and you need to have those too. I have a lead generation website for my SEO work (www.theSEOman.co.uk) where I showcase a case study where I ranked a broken website that wasn't even in Google's first 1,000 results in just 60 days. But more than that: I ranked that website in the top spot of Google, Yahoo, Bing and YouTube *within 60 days*. And if that wasn't impressive enough, I ranked the website in the SEO space, where *every competitor in an SEO*.

To the right client, this is like finding gold. I *deliberately* send SEO enquiries that come to me via other sources to *that* website, and most of the time I never hear back from them. *Because they don't understand the value of a masterpiece when they see one.*

"I see it now," said Dave. "I have a ton of clients like that," he said, pulling his face. "It's hard work serving them and they're never happy or grateful."

"Who's fault is *that*, then?" I asked him.

"Yes," he said. "I went for the entire market, instead of for those people that I can actually serve best."

"You're robbing your best clients of your best services by

spending all your resources firefighting with the wrong clients. Short term gain, lifetime of stress."

"OK, OK!" Dave put his hands up.

"OK," I smiled. "So that's *that* belief proved wrong. You can't serve the entire market anyway, so don't be scared of serving only the right people."

Now let me show you why you're wrong about the next belief too…

FALSE: My Offer is Really Not Unique
so I Can't Position it...

We were at the Apple store and my wife, Krish, picked up an iPen and showed it to me. "I need this," she told me.

I looked at it. "How much is it?"

She told me.

"What?!" I screeched. "That much *for a stylus?*"

Krish looked at me in shock, then looked at what she was holding in her hand. "It's the iPen!" she said.

"*It's a stylus!*" I cried.

Suddenly there was doubt in her. "When you put it that way..." she said, putting it down.

Your product doesn't have to be that unique. What are you sitting on? A chair? Is it unique? And your furniture at home? Is that unique? What about your tv? Is that unique? Can you tell me about anything that *is* unique? Probably very few things you own are....

When you buy 'things', you're mostly buying brands, not products. If we bought products, there would be no need for hundreds of furniture manufacturers, tv manufacturers, and just about anything you can think of. There is competition almost everywhere. Even sheds are made by multiple companies. If a unique product was a requirement, you'd never enter a market because *almost everything you can come up with is already out there.* You wouldn't, for example, be able to sell accounting services if there's already an accountant in town. So would would you do? Uproot? Good luck finding a town that doesn't have an accountant already!

And by the way, we went back for the iPen, which serves another lesson. If your positioning and your branding is powerful and compelling, you can sell almost anything - as long as it's useful or valuable to your customers. Unlike a stylus, the iPen does enhance the iPad experience, but the point of this story was that I was unable to see the value of it because I didn't know what it was (i.e. I was the wrong prospect for that offer).

If Apple released a mug with their logo on it, I'm sure it would be a success, and yet mugs are not unique. *But Apple's positioning is, and that creates loyal fans, which in turn buy everything you have to offer them if it's useful or valuable to them.*

FALSE: My Offer is Inferior to My Competitor's Offer...

Can you cook a better burger at home than a McDonald's burger? I'd be both disappointed and surprised if you answered no to this... And yet, McDonald's is a global giant. Thus, clearly *it is not about the product*. That said, a great product helps of course... but in this case, just about anybody can cook a better burger (in my opinion).

Does our friend the mobile mechanic need to be the best mechanic in the world to service our cars? No. As long as his offer solves our problem and meets our pricing point, we're happy. He services our cars whilst we work, so his offer packs a lot of value: *we save time*.

When you get your positioning right, and you create customers that appreciate you and your service, then your offers - as long as they meet their pricing points and they solve their problems - will sell.

There are over 1 million phone cases in Amazon right now, including one of my own test products. I used it as a case study to generate tons of sales in Amazon. I then moved on and focused on other projects... so that phone case is floating somewhere in Amazon - ranked in the thousands (which means you'd be lucky to find it) but whenever I run a quick ad for a few days, I get sales. People *still* buy my phone case despite the fact that there are a million choices - literally - and I don't even have brand awareness, nor do I have the best product!

FALSE: I Don't Have as Much Money as My Competitors so I Can't Compete...

How much money would you need to take on your competitors? Name the figure. Go ahead. 1 million? If I secured 1 million for you, would you *then* be confident to take on your competitors? And what exactly would you do with that 1 million? More of what you've been doing up to now?

If you don't know your numbers (your cost of sales and your conversion rate) and you don't have systems in place to measure, track and show you those numbers, then you don't have control of your business at the ROI level. So what's a million going to do for you? Not much. At best, you'll squander it with no idea of your ROI and no systems in place to test and improve your conversions as you squander that money on trying to generate new leads.

Instead, if you had a sales funnel in place where you could predictably enter 1 grand and get back a little more than what you put in... then you would have your own personal money-printing ATM machine.

So let me ask you again: how much money do you actually need to take on your competitors? Nowhere near a million, is the answer. The reality is that many business owners bootstrap this process, investing a little as they earn. So it's not about the money... it's about the systems you set up.

If you have a positive ROI in your sales funnel, then what do you care about how much money your competition has? All you need to do is keep sending visitors to *your* sales funnel and convert them positively, *because that's what's going to be putting money in your bank account.*

The other reality is that you're not really going head to head with your competitors, so it's not literally your money against theirs. Whilst your competitor targets the market as a whole, you're going to be targeting a segment of that market and serving it very well. This will help you craft your unique positioning, which in turn should make you more profitable (if you've identified the right segment in that market and they are comfortable with your pricing points) so you're not really going to have competition per se.

Still need a million?

Mr Big Pants And
The Powerful Point of Difference

"Ok," Dave acceded. "You've destroyed all my beliefs," he said, scratching his head.

"Don't feel sad about those false beliefs," I said. "You didn't know all this other stuff was out there, so it's not really your fault. You were simply operating within your realm of reality".

"Out of curiosity, what is your *point* of difference right now?"

"That's a clever question," I answered. "*Right Now* is the correct way to look at this. The market shifts and trends come and go, and the smart brands stay fluid enough to respond quickly."

Dave looked pleased with himself.

"Right now, I'm in different markets, so I have different positioning, but to give you a good example of how I'm exploiting bigger agencies that have multiple employees in the online marketing space, let me ask you a question…"

"Sure," Dave nodded. "Ask away."

"Imagine you're going to hire a company to help promote your website. You search online and you find Big Pants Awesome Online Marketing Ltd. They're not the cheapest, of course, but you already know that you get what you pay for, and you want the best that you can afford. Big Pants is good enough and just about within your budget - they're the best your current budget can buy. So tell me, why are you going to go with Big Pants?"

Dave thought about this. "Well," he said. "They have a proven track record," he grinned, getting into the role play. "They have lot of testimonials and clients, so I have confidence in them."

"So you'll pay a higher premium for Big Pants to handle your marketing?"

"Yes," Dave nodded.

"Well," I said. "Mr Big Pants has come a long way since his early days. He's a specially good marketer, and that's enabled him to build a big agency on the back of his successes. But he's no longer personally working on client's campaigns. He has no time for that. He has staff now, and he has delegated those tasks. In fact, he's now scaling his company and taking on new staff, but good marketers are expensive *(that's why we start our own companies, because we're good...)* and in order to scale he needs more bums on seats. He has 2 choices: outsource the work to a different company or employ interns or apprentices.

If he outsources, he's not going to use a company here, because the cost will squeeze out his profit margin. Instead, he will probably look at emerging economies and hire people there. But it takes time to vet people.. and I'm sure Mr Big Pants is not going to be training *any* strangers abroad, let alone giving away his magic sauce.

So what does that leave you with? Let's see: you pay premium prices for marketing, because Mr Big Pants is leveraging *his* personal success via his brand. But Mr Big Pants is not working on your marketing campaign. Instead, an apprentice is. So, you're paying top prices for an inexperienced apprentice to handle your marketing."

Dave pulled his face. "When you put it that way…"

"It's a hypothetical example," I say. "I'm not suggesting anybody works like this, and I'm sure that the apprentice would have the right resources at his or her disposal - not to mention the ability to ask for help - to manage your campaign properly.

B*ut that's not what I'm asking*. I'm asking: *if you knew* an apprentice who works for a big firm is going to be handling your marketing, would you pay 3 times a much than you would, let's say, an experienced online marketer that will work on your campaign personally?"

"I see what you mean," Dave said, thoughtfully. "It makes you think, really…"

"*This* is precisely the gap I'm exploiting," I said. "My unique positioning is that despite my experience of over a decade marketing online and having worked with clients in 21 countries, *I still deal with every single client 1 on 1*. Personally. Somebody else answers the phone unless my mobile rings, but I speak with the client personally before *anything* happens, and - more importantly - I personally design and craft and execute and manage their advertising campaigns and sales funnels and anything else."

"That's a powerful USP," Dave agreed.

"Thank you," I replied. "On the one hand, my positioning limits how many clients I can take on, but on the other it enables me to provide more value to those clients I do agree to work with. *And this gives the client the biggest value.*"

Dave clapped. "I like it. Can I borrow it?"

"Of course. Take it. Use it. Every one person company that's driven by a person who has experience has this same edge: the fact that the small company can't take on staff *is their advantage when they leverage this and make it a part of their unique positioning.*"

"I'm not saying I will use this positioning forever," I added, "but for now - *or at least for a limited time* - everybody gets to work with me 1 on 1."

"You've given me all I need," said Dave. "I get it now. I need to identify who I want to serve in my market, then find the gaps that the competition is creating and reposition myself, or better position myself to fully exploit them. That will automatically make my offer unique. The more gaps I can exploit, the more unique I become, until my competition simply vanishes and I'm left alone to serve my ideal customers like nobody else does or can. This in turn enables me to price my offers at what they're actually worth, because there's no competitors to engage me in a price war!"

"Very good. But you've forgotten one thing," I said.

"Keep watching the market for changes," Dave said. "So I can adapt and service any new gaps that appear."

"Yes," I said. "You now get The Secret of how to wipe out your competition in one move: *position yourself uniquely*. But you're forgetting something."

"Go on," Dave said. "Tell me."

"*The Machine.* Everything you need to put in place in order for your unique positioning to work for you. You don't want to be the best unique pizza shop in the middle of the desert!"

"Ah," said Dave.

"Indeed, said I.

"This sounds like a lot of work," Dave mumbled.

"It is," I agreed. "But that's what I'm here for. I'm about to give you a decade's worth of hard-earned wisdom distilled down to 7 secrets. The 7 key things you need to put in place to support your unique positioning. *How's that for a shortcut?*"

PART 2: THE 7 SECRETS

SECRET 1: YOUR OFFER

It all starts with your offer. Your offer determines the market, and your resources determine your offer. Your resources can be skills (i.e. what you can do) or access to products and services (i.e. what you can get).

If you're a carpenter and that's the core skill you wish to brand, then your offer is going to be whatever you come up with within your skillset. This can be a product (e.g. a breakfast stool) or an information product (e.g. a 'how to make your own breakfast stool' ebook or course).

When you plugin the Web to your business, the opportunities open up exponentially. The lone carpenter who faced extinction at the hand of the big furniture stores in town can now offer an online course and reach the entire globe, whereas the big furniture store doesn't have the resources (time) or the foresight - in many cases - to do this. *This is how you exploit a gap with your offer.*

Once you determine what your offer is going to be - whether skill-based or resource-based - commit to *knowing* your product well, whether you choose a physical or digital product, or both. You must be able to answer questions about your product with answers that position your product in the right way - the right way being whatever you decide your positioning should be.

For example, if your offer is resource-based (e.g. a leather phone case) and your chosen market is the business sector, then positioning your phone when answering a question about *why your product is good* could be to explain that the plush leather case is business-grade and fits well within a business environment, rather than saying *it keeps your phone safe*, which is not a feature that is exclusive to the business sector.

I once worked with a client to whom, on our first call, I asked: *why would I buy your product instead of your competitor's product?* He actually answered "*I don't know*".

I had to refrain from saying: *if you don't know, then how is your client going to know?*

His product was resource-based (he was selling a product that he was importing, and it wasn't unique in any way. I'm not saying you have to be passionate about your product (some people make good money selling shower curtain rings, and I can't imagine anybody getting passionate about those…) but *do craft answers that at least attempt to sell your product.*

You often hear online that you have to be passionate about your product. I always think of toilet paper sellers when I hear this. How passionate you are should mostly depend on your market. I like to look at this from the other end: I try to imagine how passionate the customer will be about the product. Customers don't start jumping from foot to foot and hollering when they buy toilet paper, so I - as the seller - don't need to either.

Match the customer's' passion. If they're buying a fish bowl, don't sing at them when they do, because *they're* not singing. *They just need a fish bowl.* If you're selling a stress-reducing CD, don't shout about it like those irritating sofa and car commercials on the radio, *because your customers are already one scream away from a nervous breakdown.*

Position your passion to align with your customer's passion. Otherwise you'll raise flags in your customers' minds by acting like a freak when they're not expecting you to.

SECRET 2: YOUR TARGETING

When you're clear on what your offer is, think about who your ideal customer is and what the most valuable thing you can offer them is.

For example, my ideal customer is an entrepreneur / solopreneur / business owner who knows they have a good product or service or idea but does not have the know-how to turn their business into a *brand* and promote it online and scale up without going bust. It doesn't matter if the customer is already online, or is completely online-based. I can create physical product brands for them or fix their existing product lines; I can launch them as authors or set up lead-generating machines for their businesses. What matters most to me is that they understand their own business and they're in a position to invest.

The most valuable thing I can offer my ideal customer, is my 1 on 1 service, where I personally look at their business and craft a sales funnel tailor-made for them, then implement the systems and campaigns to advertise, track, measure and improve conversion until we achieve a positive ROI. In other words, the most valuable service I can offer my ideal client is to *reposition them and / or set up their own money-printing ATM machine.*

On the other hand, my nightmare client is what I call The Duck Tape Client. These people think that they can do my job intuitively and insist on controlling everything, including the things they don't understand.

Duck Tape Clients dictate every aspect of their website and spend 5 minutes writing a blurb, then blame the web designer when the website doesn't convert. They launch untargeted ads without understanding that they need to research and segment the audience and without a clue about copywriting and then blame the web designer. It never occurs to them that it may be *them*. The reason I call them Duck Tape clients is because they dictate the strategy and then employ somebody to fix and patch bits as they get new ideas, and end up with a mess.

Spend as much time figuring out who your nightmare client is, because you need to filter this type of client out.

Once you identify your ideal client and the best thing you can offer them, craft your marketing in a way that attracts your ideal customer and repels everybody else.

In my case, there are a lot of online solopreneurs (especially people who want to sell online, or want to get into Internet marketing) who are bootstrapping their way. I started very humbly too, but I can't serve those people with the same level of value that I can serve my ideal customer, because their pricing point simply doesn't pay for the amount of time and resources I need to allocate to setting up an ATM machine. And if I did try to serve them at this level, I would be doing my high-end clients a disservice by not focusing my resources *on them*.

However, I do have *many* separate offers at much lower pricing points to serve those people who are further down the ladder. For example, my Social Media automation tool - at the time of this

writing - includes a basic version which is free. *The tool is a must for any business and entrepreneur, whether you work on or offline, and you can't get cheaper than 'free'.* So do sign up for that, whilst the offer is available. Visit my resources page and look for the social media tool:
www.untouchablebrand.com/resources

I do try to serve as many people as I can with as much value as I can, depending on what they can afford, so for those customers who can't afford the 1 on 1 but are keen to get set up, I offer a more affordable service where I create a blueprint for them to help them implement the right systems.

So think about your ideal client and the best service you can provide them with, then consider whether you can service anybody else that is further down the chain. If you're the lone carpenter with the online course, your ideal customer may be the one that's ready to pay for the 6 week course and the 1 on 1 consultation. But you can still cater to the people further down that chain by offering the course without the 1 on 1 consultation, at a lower price. And you can scale down further without compromising your resources by catering to the people who can't afford the cost of your course by implementing an instalment payment plan.

The key things to understand is who your ideal customer is, so that you can position your offer to that person, and to realise who are the people you should be *avoiding*, because *those* people will be your most expensive mistake.

SECRET 3: YOUR BRANDING

In over a decade of working with clients across dozens of industries, I've seen very few of them who understood and utilised the power of branding.

When I was setting up websites and stores for *everybody*, one of the first things I always asked for was the logo. 9 times out of a 10 the customer had no branding whatsoever. This wouldn't be a problem normally, after all, *I'm a branding specialist*, but it was, because those customers didn't come to me for branding... they came to me for a website or a store that they thought would be an instant success.

During those crazy years, I received logos that people made in MS Word, using clipart! I received hand-drawn sketches and once I even received a photograph of an embroidered badge!

It is staggering to think that all those customers who would not themselves buy something from a website that looked like the work of a drunk, thought (quite arrogantly) that *their* clipart logos would cause a buying frenzy.

Today, my ideal customer needs help with branding, but is not stupid enough to believe branding means spending as little as possible on a logo.

Start with your logo: do you have a professional logo? If your web designer created your logo then realise that branding and web design are 2 different specialties. If you bought a cheap website, the web designer may have knocked together a logo for you at your insistence to secure the job.

Today, you're wiser. Get a professional logo that reflects your positioning. Your logo is *pivotal* to your branding - it is *the face* of your brand. Don't make a joke out of all the hard work you've put into getting here by taking a shortcut and skimping on one of the most important elements of your entire brand.

SECRET 4: GET ONLINE

I still hear business owners say that the Web is not for them, that their businesses are *not really web friendly*. Sadly, that's what many high street travel agents thought. Remember those? They were everywhere. You popped inside, grabbed a brochure, chose the destination you wished to visit, sat down and waited for the employee to get you some prices.

Then the World Wide Web appeared. And they said: *it's not really for us. Our businesses are high street businesses. People walk in here... they like to leaf through the brochures and ask questions. They like the feel of paper.*

They got wiped out like the dodo.

The scary thing is that few businesses have a better target audience than '*people who want to go on holiday*' so for all intents and purposes, being a travel agent in the high street *was* a solid business model - perhaps even more solid back then than our own business are by comparison.

I still see the odd travel agent tucked away in a backstreet, but those are not mainstream: they cater to ethnic segments of the population. I wonder if they realise their shelf-life is about to expire: the offspring of those ethnic segments are Web-savvy; they're highly unlikely to visit those same travel shops their parents did when they have all the information they need at their fingertips. Time they started working on expanding their offerings into cross-markets...

I don't need to tell you about near-empty shopping centres and small town-centres in less affluent areas with boarded-up shops. Shopping and doing business online is more convenient. Even consuming news and content is more convenient online - *ask the newspapers*.

So if you happen to be one of those who say your business and the online world are not compatible, I would say *find a way to make them compatible before you get wiped out*.

If you run a funeral parlour, you may think brick-and-mortar is all you need. *But the bereaved are are looking online for quick solutions too.* You may have the most Earth-bound business in town, but the fact is that your Earthly customers are online, consuming content and looking for solutions to their problems. And if your competitors are there, providing your market with the help they need *when* they need it, like it or not, you're giving your business away to the competition.

Online is not a different world. The same people who walk into your business are the ones who are spending time online, and they're not postponing finding solutions to their problems until it's convenient for *you*. They're looking for those solutions when it's convenient *for them*. And that's usually on-the-go, via their smartphones, or in the evening when they're sat in front of the tv or in bed.

Today's consumer - and that includes us - is all-powerful, with information one finger-tap or mouse-click away. *You need to be at the end of those fingertips or that click if you want to survive.*

Being online for your prospects does not mean that you have to be physically there, taking questions and calls. Just having a presence can be enough - at the very least to establish trust with that future-customer, to assure them that you are 'there'.

Conversely, not having an online presence can hurt you for exactly the same reason. You and your competitor may be closed for business on Sunday evening, but when your prospect is on your competitor's website, consuming *their* information, guess who they're going to call in the morning if they haven't already emailed them via an online contact form?

Not you.

So, we both agree then that it's not about making the online world fit your business. It's the other way around: you must find a way to fit around the online world, to establish a bridge for those future clients, to create an open channel of communication between the working hours in which your business lives and the 24 hour day in which everybody else lives.

SECRET 5: YOUR WEBSITE & YOUR SALES COPY

Next is your website. Your website is designed around your logo, *not the other way around.* When I perform a website appraisal, one of the things I usually see is a total disconnect between the logo and the website. A Frankenstein'*ism.*

Your website is one of your best assets. It 'sells' (or 'destroys') your brand for you 24x7x365. Your potential customers will be looking at your website and what they see there is going to represent *you and your brand.* Make sure your website is modern and up-to-date.

I have legacy clients, to this day, who have websites that are *desperately* old. The systems I used back then to build those websites have long been obsolete; the websites are not mobile responsive, because back then smartphones weren't even around. I still lose sleep hosting those websites, because they are exploitable by 3rd grade hackers and just about any rudimentary hacking tool out there. They are ticking bombs.

A hacked or infected website can cause tremendous damage to your reputation and can turn into a lengthy and costly event for you. Make sure you're protected. Invest in the security of your website and don't be the client that thinks *it won't happen to me.* Invest in SSL (the green padlock that protects you user's data) and get an antivirus solution on your website, as well as a good security audit and plan in place. Your visitors will take your brand seriously when you do, not before.

I began writing a book years ago, titled *The 3 Year Website*. It was based around the odd fact that business owners who have a car on a payment plan, swap the car for a new model every 3 years or so. They also change their suits more regularly than that, because they understand that visuals are important, especially in business. And yet, they have Stone Age websites flying the flag for their company.

Since then, the exponential growth of technology and the influx of new platforms and tools to work with has been tremendous, so much so that upgrading a website every 3 years now is - in most cases - too slow. I have changed my corporate website a dozen times in the last two years, and whilst I accept that I am able to do this for myself, I have better things to do than to change my website around every few months. In other words, I'm not changing my website around because I can. I'm changing it *because I have to.*

Stay modern. Your visitors are visiting you *in the now*, so don't give them a 2001 experience unless you want them to be wowed by your competitor's website instead. Close that exploitable gap before your competitor sees it.

Finally, when your website *design* is complete, it's time to craft your sales pages. Don't think that spending 5 minutes writing *anything* will get you anywhere. I've worked with hundreds of clients over the years, and almost every one of them hated writing. If you don't like writing, *hire somebody to write the sales copy on your website!* You get out what you put in, so if you want a million dollar brand, treat it *and build it* like a million dollar brand.

SECRET 6: GET SOCIAL

Your customers are social, period. At the time of this writing, Facebook has 1.5 billion users. But that's not the only place where your customer can hang out. LinkedIn, Twitter, Pinterest, Instagram and just about any new platform that appears can host some of your potential customers. *And they have no idea about you and your brand.*

All those potential customers are *one click away from you.* Facilitate that click by posting content online. Blog and use Social Media networks to get your message out there and put your brand in front of countless potential customers and an ever-growing audience.

If you're shaping yourself to be a future celebrity or thought leader in your space, then the core messages need to come from you - *but not necessarily all the content.* If you're building a team, then the message can be a collaboration. If on the other hand you have no time for Social Media, then pay a professional to handle this for you. Realise that this arena is where your brand can get the most traction at the most affordable price point.

If you're bootstrapping this, then go for it, but realise that what you put out there *reflects your brand and its values,* and in Social Media *it doesn't usually go away.* So be very careful not to mix your channels and upset your customers because that can impact your business in a negative way.

Once you're clear on what your core message is, be consistent.

Nothing is more off-putting to a Social Media savvy visitor that checks out your online channels than seeing that your last post was 2 years ago, and was '*hello*'.

Be everywhere. Utilize all the major Social Media platforms - the ones that *everybody else* is using - and make sure your brand is part of that conversation.

Provide value. Don't self-promote over and over. Provide value to your audience. Give them a reason to stay engaged. Providing relevant value is how your demonstrate your authority.

Managing all your activity can be a nightmare. My Social Media tool provides you with a convenient dashboard where you can create and schedule content for each of the main platforms. The Pro account tracks your content and provides you with key metrics so that you can see how many times your content was clicked and what times that activity took place. This enables you to see what content is resonating with your audience and what the best times to post that content are. Using this powerful tool you can hone in and start creating fabulous content that your audience laps up, and deliver it at the optimal time.
Check out my resources page and look for The Social Media tool: www.untouchablebrand.com/resources

SECRET 7: ADVERTISE, OPTIMISE & SCALE

Once you have your branding right and you've positioned yourself to serve your chosen audience uniquely, it's time to start advertising. There are many ways to advertise and some will prove to be better than others for different brands targeting different markets with different offers. Test as many as you can and watch the results closely.

Back when I used to deal with *the wrong clients*, I would end up having to explain how online advertising works. I would start by explaining that essentially, there are two types of advertising: organic (SEO = getting your web pages ranked in the search engines) and paid (pay-per-click = you create an ad and it appears on the first page).

As soon as I explained pay-per-click, the client would rush off to try it. The striking thing is that copywriters spend a lifetime dedicated to learning and improving the art of crafting effective sales copy (did you know that the people who write the headlines in newspapers are not the same people who write the articles? Headline writers get paid a lot more...) but these clients usually decided that they were what I now call Instant Masters of Sales Copy.

Not surprisingly, those clients would often return, beaten, complaining that they'd been fleeced by the search engine's advertising platform, and declaring that pay-per-click advertising doesn't work.

When this happens, I always ask the same question: did people click the ads? *Everybody did*, they always say (after all, that's where the ad cost came from). *And nobody bought anything!* They always complain.

If everybody clicked the ads, I always reply, *then the ads were a raging success. What else can they do, other than click your ad?*

This answer is always greeted with silence. And then, I usually hear *but nobody bought anything!*

That's because the web page they see *after the ad is clicked* is what sells the offer, *not the ad.* And as you've probably guessed, these people wrote *anything* as fast as they could to put on those pages, with the intention of never revising that page to tweak what they wrote.

Incidentally, these are Duck Tape clients. Although I no longer work with this type of client, I do sometimes speak with them and on the odd occasion try to give them a little nudge in the right direction… but it never works.

I had a client who told me that he had paid for an ad and sent people to his offer, and nobody bought. I asked him how many people he had sent via that ad, expecting to hear at least 100. The answer was less than 20.
Less than 20.

I explained that at the very least he should wait to get 100 visitors to see the offer page. I like to get 1,000 before I start making decisions, so 100 is a bare minimum. From there, work out your conversion rate. If 1 person buys or becomes a lead, then you have a 1% conversion rate. Start there and work upwards.

No, the client explained. *I didn't understand. This was a good offer. It was impossible that people wouldn't buy.*

Incredible. You just can't beat an Instant Master. Without seeing any of what he did, I would take a guess and say that his ad was poor and targeted *everybody* (e.g. Great BBQ). How many people who clicked on that ad do you think would *not* have been quality leads or even aligned to the offer? Most, I can tell you. Next, out of the very few potential *real* leads or buyers that came through, how many do you think were stupefied by the poorly written offer page?

Master copywriters charge thousands of dollars per hour to craft sales copy, and they get excited at a 20% to 30% conversion rate (that's seriously good!) but The Instant Master / Duct Tape client expects more from his 5 minute effort.

I tell *you* all this to save you money and heartache by showing you where others went wrong. *Nobody is making me write this book. I'm writing this because I want you to succeed by understanding what needs to be in place and why it needs to be done properly.*

Being aware of one's limitations is a good skill to have. Hire a professional to do the important pieces that you don't have the skill to do. If advertising is one of those skills you lack, either learn to advertise or invest in an a professional. Just *don't do what the Instant Masters do.*

The last piece of the puzzle is optimising: this means optimising everything in your sales funnel, from your content to your advertising to your offer pages and everything in between. It means split testing offers, headlines, bullet points, images and more.

Think of this as winner-stays-on in a game of pool. Your original offer is called *the control.* Create a variation, called *the test*, and send 50% of your visitors to one offer page and the other 50% to the other page, and then measure results. Your job is to beat the control. When the test wins by converting more visitors, the test becomes the control and you create a new variation to test, *but now your conversions are better than they were before.* The trick is to keep improving your conversion using this winner-stays-on approach.

Measure everything, from ad spend to click-through rate (how many people click the ads) to visits to conversions, and figure out your cost of sales (how much it costs you to make a sale). Once you know all this, you know how much you can afford to spend acquiring a new customer whilst still being profitable. If your cost of sales (CoS) is £10 at break-even then you can afford to spend *almost* £10 to acquire a lead without losing money. You can then increase your profit per customer by designing and implementing a well-crafted sales funnel that takes your new acquisitions through relevant offers. Think McDonald's.

Testing and measuring is an ongoing process.

Is it tedious? It can be. Is it necessary? You tell me: if you sell a £250 service and your conversion rate is 1% (1 in a 100 people buy) and it's costing you £200 to buy 100 visitors, then you have your own ATM machine by definition, but if you haven't started split-testing then what you have is a situation where you're leaving a lot of money on the table without even knowing it. Let's say you spend the time testing headlines and other elements, and you increase your conversion rate to 3%, which is reasonably achievable in many markets...

... this means you now make £750 instead of £250 *from the same 100 visitors.* In other words, your ad spend didn't go up because you didn't buy new visitors. *You're still spending £200 in advertising but now you're making 3 times as much as you were before you started testing*!

Business owners who don't realise this, typically set up an offer on a page (i.e. a website) and forget about it. Mostly, they don't even advertise, so nobody ever sees the page.

Conversion optimisation is where the riches are made. If you follow the steps in this book and position yourself to serve a specific segment of your market in a unique way, craft your branding *deliberately and professionally,* set up a website that reflects the quality of your brand, craft your sales funnel and your offers utilizing good sales copy, start promoting your message via social networks and by creating valuable content and run smart advertising campaigns to drive people to your offers, then all that's left to do is to test and test and keep testing the key elements in your offer and your landing pages to strategically and methodically improve the conversion rate of your offer. This will lower your advertising costs by generating more money from the same amount of visitors.

This is how you set up a money-printing ATM machine and position yourself in a way that simultaneously wipes out your competition from your chosen segment and enables you to increase your price points.

PART 3 - WRAPPING IT UP & MY RESOURCES

HOW MUCH DOES IT COST
TO BUILD YOUR OWN ATM MACHINE?

"Ok," said Dave, excitedly. "You've convinced me. I see things differently now, because *now* I know that certain things exists that I can use, like tracking my ROI to the penny. So let me ask you... how much does this cost? How much would it cost to build me an ATM machine?"

"That's the wrong question," I answer. "If you see this as a cost, then you're not seeing this at all.

The mortgage on a 12-apartment complex is over 100 times the cost of my home mortgage, so by that logic, you would never consider it. But that would be to ignore the fact that a home - whilst you live in it - is not an asset, it's a liability. *It doesn't generate money*. Whereas the 12-apartment complex brings in 11 lots of rent (if you choose to live in one) every single month, consistently. So price is *never* the question. *There is a cost to everything*.

There is a cost to run a business, there is a cost to passing up an opportunity. The only question that matters is *how profitable is it?* If it's making profit, *does the cost matter?*

"My bad," Dave says, nodding. "So..."

I smile. "You've taken in a lot of new good stuff. Things that you didn't know where available. Digest it. Get used to the idea that there are new rules, and think about how vulnerable you are in your market when you have competitors who have more resources than you do.

Go to my resources page and see what tools you can use, if you want to take the DIY approach."

And if you need my help, you know where I am...

ABOUT DAVE

Meet Dave. Dave is a plumber, a dentist, a blogger, an accountant, an Amazon seller, a landscape gardener, a seller of appliances, a kitchen company owner, a small enterprise owner...

He has the same pride-driven stubbornness we all have when it comes to taking advice about our businesses, and that same blind spot we all have when it comes to identifying gaps that he's creating in his own market, *for competitors to exploit*.

But it's not really his fault. Dave only knows what he knows. He didn't know, for example, that there are systems that enable you to track ROI instead of having to blindly pour money into advertising. He didn't even realise you could set up your own ATM machine.

Times are *fast* now. These are The New Rules. Knowing how to position your brand to remove the competition and understanding The 7 Secrets before others in your market are even aware...

... gives you a unique and powerful edge.

ABOUT MY RESOURCES

The tools I use day to day change often. New tools enter the
market and others simply disappear. The speed of *change* online
today is staggering, and so in order to keep this book as up-to-
date as possible, I decided to list my resources on my website,
where I can update them as and when I discover new tools to
work with.

You can find that page here:
www.untouchablebrand.com/resources

Thank you for allowing me to share my journey with you. I hope
you enjoyed it and I hope you got a lot of value from it. I've given
you 10 years of distilled experience gained from working mostly
in the digital space, where the speed of change and my addiction
to learning various key disciplines as well as the good fortune to
be able to work with hundreds of clients across many markets
has enabled me to see and learn what may have taken me a
lifetime to experience in the offline world.

Use this before the rules change again.

Jose M. Gonzalez Riley